COME AS
You Are

Sandra Valentino

ISBN 978-1-68570-069-0 (paperback)
ISBN 978-1-68570-070-6 (digital)

Christian Faith Publishing
832 Park Avenue
Meadville, PA 16335
www.christianfaithpublishing.com

Printed in the United States of America

Preface

There are many stories of God's miraculous healings done for perfect Christians. This is *not* one of those stories. This story is about the miraculous healing he did for me, a sinner! I'm sure it is one of many that the world never hears about. My accident was over fifteen years ago, and I am still amazed today by the miracles and blessings God gave me throughout our nineteen-month journey together. He didn't just give me one miracle and everything was fixed—he went on the journey with me. He gave me one small miracle after the next, until I was restored to good physical health and even better spiritual health. Along the way, he tested me so I would have a testimony! He allowed me to feel the pain but never more than I could bear! He always showed me that there was hope so I wouldn't give up! He worked through my doctors and nurses, but I could always feel God's presence and knew he was guiding them and working through them.

Introduction

D o you ever feel like you're not good enough to go to God? Like you are required to wait until you are a better person? Do you believe that you should postpone it until you have your life in order and you are no longer a sinner before you attend church regularly or pray the prayer of salvation or even get baptized? Do you feel like you cannot pray to God because you are unworthy? Do you think that, maybe, it will be easier to be a Christian when you are married and settled down so there will be less peer pressure and temptations? These are all lies that the enemy tells you to keep you from experiencing the amazing love of your heavenly Father.

Christians are never perfect! We are also never too far from God to ask for his mercy and forgiveness. You can come to Jesus just as you are; you just can't stay there. But with Jesus, it is so natural to learn and grow because he is helping you and guiding you to become the person that he created you to be. Without Jesus, it is nearly impossible. God does not withhold his miracles from you simply because you are not perfect or you're not growing in your faith fast enough. Even if you backslide, God never gives up on you!

According to John 3:16–18:

> For this is how God loved the
> world: He gave his one and only Son, so

that everyone that believes in him will not perish but have eternal life. God sent His Son into the world not to judge the world, but to save the world through Him. There is no judgement against anyone who believes in him.

I believe these verses tell us that we are not perfect but we are loved and forgiven!

HOW JESUS FOUND US!

I am the youngest of five girls. My parents were Lutheran, and my mom would take us to church every Sunday. The church taught us that if we were good, we would go to heaven. My mom truly believed everything she was taught. She was a fourth-grade Sunday school teacher for many years. All my sisters completed catechism. We never missed an Ash Wednesday or Palm Sunday service. We were not permitted to eat meat on Fridays during lent. My mom did her best to ensure that we all followed the teachings of the church.

We didn't find out what the Bible truly says about salvation until my sister, Lori, married a marine and he was stationed in California. While Lori and Glenn were living in California, they met a good Christian woman who shared the message of salvation with them. She explained to them that the Bible says in John 3:3 that unless a man is born again, he will not see the kingdom of heaven. She explained that if you confess with your mouth that Jesus is Lord and believe in your heart that God raised him from the dead, you shall be saved (Romans 10:9–10). It is only by God's grace that we are saved (Ephesians 2:9). Lori and Glenn prayed the prayer of salvation and brought the truth home to Pennsylvania where the rest of the family slowly followed their lead. You can read their testimony in the back of this book.

I prayed the prayer of salvation and invited Jesus into my heart when I was thirteen years old. I attended Christian school in eighth and ninth grade, not because I was the good little Christian girl—it was because I was getting into too much trouble in public school. I completed Bible courses as part of the curriculum. I wanted to go back to public school to complete high school, and I promised my parents I would behave, so they agreed to it. Although I knew what the Bible said and what God expected of me and I had every intention of following it, I did not follow his ways.

As soon as I got back into the secular environment, I went right back to my old ways. I got in trouble in high school. I skipped class, got into fights, got drunk, and quit school the day I turned sixteen. I had premarital sex and become pregnant with my first child when I was seventeen years old. I became pregnant with my second child while planning my wedding to their father when I was eighteen years old. I was married with two children when I was only nineteen years old. I was far from the perfect Christian, not because I didn't believe or fear God but because I didn't make wise choices. I felt guilty about it all the time—apparently, not guilty enough to change it. You don't really see the importance of having a Christian husband until you marry a non-Christian and have kids with them. My husband was not a Christian, and it did not create problems in our relationship until after the kids were born. He did not see the need to go to church or take our children to church. I, on the other hand, thought that it was very important to take them and have them learn about God and what his Word says. Proverbs 22:6 reads, "Direct your children onto the right path, and when they are older, they will not leave it." I would try to take them, but it was usually too difficult for me to get myself and two babies up and ready for church, so we missed pretty many Sundays. Over the next few years, our differences in faith and how to treat and raise our children created huge problems in our marriage, and we were divorced when our children were four and five years old.

My children and I moved back in with my parents. My mother would take my kids to church with her every Wednesday night and put them in the children's program there. I continued to try to get them to church on Sunday mornings, but it never became a regular routine. I always had something more important to do, even if it was just to sleep in one day of the week. It is amazing how easily you can come up with any excuse to skip church on a Sunday morning! Honestly, I still don't make it a habit to attend church every Sunday faithfully. I listen to sermons online, and I listen to praise music in the car and at home. I talk to Jesus all day every day! He is my best friend! I'm not saying that you shouldn't attend a church and spend time with other Christians. I'm saying that being a Christian is not about going to church or even reading the Bible—it's about having a relationship with Jesus!

THE DAY JESUS SAVED MY LIFE

About a year after the divorce, I remarried. My parents had decided to take early retirement from their employers, build a home in Bradford County, Pennsylvania, and move to the mountains to enjoy their retirement. My husband and I were planning on buying their existing home when they made the move 150 miles away. They asked some friends and family to help them move all their belongings and planned to do it on Mother's Day weekend of 2003. Our family is remarkably close, and we do everything in large groups, so there ended up being about twenty-five people staying at their house for the weekend to help my parents.

Saturday, May 10, 2003, is a day that I will never forget. All the adults, except me (I am the baby of the family, and somebody had to supervise my nephew), were helping my parents with the move. My nephew (Jared), two of his friends

(Matt and Allen), and I were riding ATVs on the trails on my parents' property. They owned 111 acres, and my father had made trails all through the woods for the kids and grandkids to ride on when they came to visit. We were getting bored with the trails on the property, so we decided to go for a ride off the property. I have been riding motorcycles and ATVs in Bradford County since I was five years old. This was not something new. It was the norm for our family—just another day of riding around the mountain.

While discussing where we wanted to go for the ride, Matt mentioned that he didn't want to ride the trails because his ATV wasn't running properly and he was afraid that it would break down in the woods. He wanted to go for a ride on the dirt roads where we could take a truck if he had a problem so we could get his ATV back to the house. I did not want to ride the roads, so I told Matt he should just go with me on my ATV. Of course, a nineteen-year-old male did not want to get on the back of a twenty-eight-year-old female's ATV, so I agreed to let him drive and I would go on the back. Matt worked at an ATV dealer and was a very experienced rider. Jared decided to go on the back of Allen's ATV.

While we were getting our helmets and riding gear on and preparing to leave for our ride, my husband was arguing with me about something and my kids were fighting with each other and I was just stressed out! So when they asked me which way I wanted to go, I said, "I don't care where we go, just get me out of here."

A little while into the ride, I realized that we were going to an area of the mountain that I don't usually go to, and I asked them if they were sure if they knew the trails over there. They assured me that they found some good trails when they came up snowmobiling over the winter and they knew where they were going. So I said okay, and we continued our ride.

A couple hours later, we realized that the trails looked completely different with leaves on the trees and no snow on the ground and none of us knew where we were or how to get back to my parents' house. We were also running low on gas, so we felt we had no choice but to attempt to take the dirt roads back. We were riding on the roads for a long time, following the few road signs that are up there with arrows toward the town my parents live in. At one point, we followed a sign and, thirty minutes later, returned to the same sign! It was one big loop! This made us even more nervous about finding our way back.

Finally, Matt and I started to recognize some things and we were somewhat confident that we were going the right direction. But as a precaution, we agreed that if we saw another road sign, we were going to stop and make sure we were actually going the correct way. Eventually, we did see a sign. We stopped, read the sign, told Allen and Jared to keep following us because we knew where we were now and that we will be back to the house soon.

Now that all the stress and worrying about being lost and running out of gas was finally over, I could relax and enjoy my ride. It was a beautiful day; the weather was perfect for riding. There wasn't a cloud in the sky. It wasn't too hot to ride with riding gear on, and we weren't cold—it was just perfect. Through the woods, over a small embankment, I could see a pleasant stream running along the dirt road. I remember thinking, *I absolutely love this!* Riding has always been a way for me to forget all of life's worries and stresses and just enjoy the ride and the beautiful country!

The relaxing came to an immediate halt when the brakes locked up. I looked forward to see why Matt was braking. I saw a Chevrolet Blazer directly in front of us, but Matt was braking and we were in a controlled skid going around the

Blazer and I was sure he was going to miss it—it was really close, but I could see sunlight between the two vehicles, until the Blazer turned directly into us. The woman driving the Blazer was completely in the wrong lane when she came over the crest of the hill. There were several potholes in her lane, so she was going around them. The reconstructive expert determined that Matt could see her for 1.6 seconds before impact. There were trees to the right, the blazer directly in front of us, and her empty lane of travel when he saw her. Thank God for Matt's quick judgment and excellent reactions. My family and I truly believe that his age and years of experience definitely played a role in saving my life. If he would have chosen any of the other options, we would probably both be dead. Apparently, she attempted to return to her lane of travel as well, which was our only escape route when she hit us.

When the Blazer struck the ATV, my body was thrown into the vehicle and then hurled fifty feet through the woods where I landed and laid unconscious and gargling. Matt was launched off of the ATV also, but his body did not collide with the Blazer. He landed in a ditch on the side of the roadway. Although he had an extreme fracture in his femur—the largest bone in your body—he was conscious and alert. He just could not move because of the severe pain from the fracture in his leg. The woman who hit us was not injured. She immediately left the scene to go call 911 at a neighboring house. Fortunately, Allen and Jared were able to avoid impact with the vehicle, even though they were following only a few feet behind us. Jared and Allen went to check Matt first. He told them he was okay and they should go check me because he could hear me making a noise he had never heard before and he did not know where I was. They had to walk up a small embankment before they could see my body lying in the woods. Allen was familiar with the gurgling or death rattle. The last person he saw do that passed away before help arrived. He immediately laid hands on me and prayed! The death rattle stopped, but I was saying, "I just want to go," repeatedly. Allen begged me not to go and told me to think about Jess and Jake, my kids, who needed their mother. I eventually stopped, focused, and said, "Get me out of here, my kids need me."

After watching me hit a vehicle and fly fifty feet before landing in the woods, Allen didn't think it was a good idea to move me—not to mention that my right leg had been cut to the bone from about four inches above my knee to four inches below my knee and all the skin rolled to the back of my leg. He could see my muscles, tendons, and bones. My left leg was broken top and bottom, and he could see the bones pushing on my skin. There was a spot of blood on my sweatshirt, near my right elbow, but he did not know how serious the injury was under my sleeve. I had a brand-new helmet on that day, and there were small divots out of it from hitting the blazer and the windshield. He did not know if I suffered any head, neck, or back injuries.

I was not interested in following Allen's instructions. I wanted to get out of those woods. He told me that I tried for a long time to get my helmet open with my left hand. When I finally got the strap open, I just hit the helmet off my head. Then I wanted to get up off the ground. I told him that if he wouldn't help me, I would do it myself. When I attempted to move, it was so excruciatingly painful that I squeezed his arm so tightly and my nails made him bleed. Then he bent down by me so he could hear what I was saying. I grabbed his neck and tried to move again; it was just as painful as the first time, and he had scabs on his neck where my nails dug in. We did not know that my entire right arm was crushed. My ulnar nerve was surrounded by bone fragments. Every time

I attempted to move my arm, it was like hitting your funny bone a thousand times!

When 911 was called, they informed us that it would be forty-five minutes until help arrived because we were in such a remote location. By the grace of God, there were four emergency medical technicians on scene, working on Matt and me within fifteen minutes! They happened to be in the area, finishing another call, when our call came in. They did everything they needed to do to prepare both of us for transport to the hospital. An ambulance came to the scene and took Matt and I to meet the medivac. The medivac flew us to the first hospital. I do not remember one minute of the helicopter ride, but Matt told me I was screaming in pain the entire flight.

I don't remember much of the next ten days. I remember feeling God's presence and begging him to heal me so my children could have a mother. I was just so weak. I felt like I couldn't do anything. I couldn't even wake up. I was told that when they asked me what happened at the hospital after my surgeries, I looked at my body and said, "I remember sliding toward a Blazer. I guess we hit it." I did not remember anything from the accident scene, either of the two medivac flights or the first hospital they took me to.

After examining me, the doctor determined that my injuries were too severe to be treated at that hospital. He requested that I be flown to a high-level trauma hospital. Lehigh Valley Hospital was the number one trauma hospital in the region, so I was able to be flown there for treatment. My diagnosis was severe multiple trauma. The first hospital I was taken to was four hours away from my home. The second one was only thirty minutes—another bonus from God!

Chapter 3

THE FIRST HOSPITAL STAY

When I arrived at Lehigh Valley Hospital, Dr. McDaid and Dr. Hawkins, who happened to be on call that night, were there waiting for me. Dr. McDaid performed the surgery to repair my arm while Dr. Hawkins performed the surgery to repair my legs. My right arm required a metal plate from my shoulder to my elbow, eight screws to hold my elbow together, a metal plate from my elbow to my wrist, and pins across my hand. My left leg required metal rods placed inside the bones, which they inserted through my knee, and my right leg required stitches to put the skin back where it belonged. Dr. Hawkins later informed me that when I was brought into the hospital, he could place his entire hand over my knee and not touch any skin. I also had a few fractured ribs, which did not require surgery.

I passionately believe that it was a blessing from God that I had these two excellent surgeons. Not only are they both extremely talented but they are genuinely great people. When you get flown into a hospital emergency room, you do not get an option of who is going to operate on you, but if I did have options, I would have chosen them!

The accident occurred at approximately 7:00 p.m. on Saturday, May 10. I did not go into surgery until 6:00 a.m. on Sunday, May 11, and did not wake up from surgery until 10:00 p.m. that day. Sunday was also Mother's Day. My children, who were nine and eleven years old at the time, did not get to see their mother on Mother's Day. Not only did they not get to see me but they were not sure if I was dead or alive. They were told that I just had a broken leg, but they overheard my father tell the family that he didn't think they would ever see me alive again.

When I asked my daughter what she did when she heard her grandfather say that, she replied, "I went upstairs and cried and prayed for you, Mommy."

This just amazed me! She was eleven years old. There were twenty-five people at the house that she could have talked to, but she chose to go upstairs alone and pray for me! It was exceedingly difficult for me to deal with the fact that I was not the one responsible for teaching her about God and the power of prayer. My mother did this for her! My mother took her to church every week where she was taught to trust Jesus, her heavenly Father. Although I wasn't the one to instill this in her, I was definitely the one to reap the benefits of her prayers.

After surgery, I was placed in ICU on life support. Children under sixteen years of age were not permitted in that area, so my children were still not able to see me. I could not speak because of the breathing tube, but I was desperately trying to communicate something to my mother. She knew I would want my children and assumed that was what I was trying to convey to her. As a result, my mother repeatedly told the nurses that I needed to see my children and begged them to allow them to come. On Tuesday, a nurse finally agreed to allow my children in to see me for ten minutes when they took my breathing tube out to change it. My mother went to my children's school immediately and got them out early to bring them to see me. They both gave me their Mother's Day gifts in the ICU department of Lehigh Valley Hospital. That is the only ten minutes I remember of the first ten days! I remember fighting so hard to stay awake and read the Mother's Day cards they brought to me. I spent the next four weeks in the hospital.

Chapter 4

MY FAMILY COMES THROUGH FOR ME

The doctors informed my family that I would not be released from the hospital unless I had a bedroom and bathroom on the first floor, which I did not have. My father immediately drew up blueprints, got a building permit, gathered his friends and our family, and went to work building an addition for me. As soon as I was released from the ICU, my mother started bringing my children to the hospital to visit every day. They would take turns lying on my bed with me for thirty minutes each. I'm not sure how enjoyable it was for them because they were afraid that if they moved, they would hurt me. I had broken bones on both sides of my body, IVs, tubes, and they looked horrible.

I am truly blessed to have the family that God chose for me to be born into. My parents gave up their retirement in the mountains and moved back home to help me. My father worked on the addition from morning until night every day while my mother took care of my children and spent the time, while they were in school, at the hospital with me. In addition to my parents, my four sisters would each call every day and ask if I needed anything. I would always tell them that I was fine and didn't need anything, but they would show up anyway and do anything in their power to try to make me feel better. They would wash my hair, shave my legs, put makeup on me, and help me get dressed—all the things you can't do for yourself while lying in a hospital bed with nine broken bones.

The four weeks in a hospital were the worst! I had a shot injected in my stomach every morning to avoid getting blood clots. I would have hours of physical and occupational therapy every day. I could never come up with any excuses that worked to get out of going to it, even though I tried! Not only was it excruciatingly painful but it was also so frustrating because I had to learn to do so many basic things with nine broken bones! It made it worse that my right arm and left leg were injured. This made it impossible to use crutches or a walker; therefore, I was in a wheelchair from May until the end of July. I couldn't use the wheelchair properly either. I had to use my left arm and right leg to move it. I wasn't too upset about that though because at least I could move on my own sometimes, after somebody helped me into the wheelchair.

Every day, a nurse would come get me from my room and take me to physical therapy. There we would work on strength and flexibility in my broken leg and learn how to maneuver my wheelchair. They also taught me how to do steps safely with all my injuries. Physical therapy was for one hour each day. The worst pain was in my knee, which always amazed me because I didn't actually injure my knee. They simply inserted the rods through it. I did find out later that I had a torn meniscus as well, which was causing some of the pain, but it was still excruciating even after the surgery to fix that.

After physical therapy, I went for an hour of occupational therapy. There they would work on strength and flexibility in my shattered right arm and hand. The first time I remember waking up in the hospital, my right arm was tied to the bed rail, so I could not move it while I was sleeping, and my fingers on that hand had very little movement. Two days after my surgery to repair my arm, my elbow dislocated. The doctor thought it must be from the little bit of movement in my bed because I was heavily medicated and I wasn't out of my bed at all. They took me back in surgery to reset my elbow and then tied my arm to the bed rail so it could heal without me moving it. The therapy to get all of my fingers from stuck straight to completely bent was the worst pain I remember. I could not figure out how the pain could go all the way up to my shoulder just from slightly bending my little pinky finger. After working on my hand, they would go to my arm and attempt to make it rotate my hand up and down. Then they would move to my elbow and try to get that to bend and straighten. Finally, they would move to my shoulder and try to get my arm to lift over my head.

Another thing they work on in occupational therapy is teaching you things to make you as self-sufficient as possible when you are released from the hospital. They would have you do things like dressing yourself, folding laundry, putting dishes away—basic things that you would have to do when you returned home. Most of these things were very easy and not painful. I enjoyed this part of therapy more than any other part.

Although the therapy was long and very painful, it was definitely worth it. When I think about how bad I was, when

I was being pushed in there in my wheelchair, to how good I was, when I was walking out of there, I am completely amazed. The therapists were just wonderful people. They did have compassion for their patients, but they also knew that they were not doing them any favors by not making them do the work to get better. They were always motivating and encouraging.

Every day, my doctors would come to my hospital room for their rounds. The last week or so, I would literally cry and beg them to let me go home to my children. Every day, they would tell me that I can't go yet and try to think of reasons I should want to stay. One of them said, "You don't want to go out there. Look out the window, it's raining."

It seemed like it rained the entire time I was in there and only stopped a few days that entire summer. I didn't care if it was a flood, a tornado, or torrential downpours—I just wanted to go home! Finally, the day came that they said they were going to release me! I was never so happy in my life!

Every day that I spent in the hospital, Jess would say, "I miss you, Mommy."

I would cry because I not only missed them but I felt so guilty lying in a hospital bed for weeks, instead of being at home taking care of my children. Then I would ask Jake if he missed me too.

He would reply, "No, I'm fine."

When I was finally being released, I said, "Jake, Mommy's coming home today, but I guess you don't care because you didn't even miss me."

He replied, "Yes, I did, Mommy! I didn't tell you because I didn't want to make you cry!"

He was nine years old, and he was being strong for his mother!

When I told my mother about this, she said, "I know. Every day, when we left the hospital, he would yell at Jess and say, 'Stop making Mommy cry! Tell her you don't miss her!'"

I guess that is the logic of a nine-year-old boy who is worried about his mommy!

Chapter 5

THE SECOND HOSPITAL STAY

I was released from the hospital early enough in the day to go to Jess's field day at school that afternoon. She was so happy to have me there, even though I looked so bad; I think I scared the other kids. The next morning was Jake's field day at school. He was just as happy to have me there watching him! I was so grateful to be home and doing what moms should do for their children—well, not everything moms do but as much as I physically could. At least I was there to support each of them. I love when they look to see if you were watching after they do something that they know you will be proud of.

After leaving Jake's field day, I went directly to my first appointment for outpatient therapy. First, I had physical therapy. They did their evaluation and began some therapy on my legs. It went as well as could be expected. Next, I went to occupational therapy. They began their evaluation of my arm. Then they unwrapped the bandages to do the wound care. As soon as the bandages were off, the therapist said, "I can see your metal."

Another therapist was walking by and said, "Oh yeah, I see it."

I could not see the back of my arm, but I was thinking it must be bad if that person can see it while walking past. They never even stopped. The therapist called my surgeon, and they instructed my mother to take me back to the hospital immediately!

I begged my mother not to take me back there. I had just been released the day before. Of course my mother didn't agree with me that it was a horrible idea to take me back there. So I started calling every person I could think of to come pick me up! I was shocked when every single person I called told me that they would not pick me up and that I had to go back in the hospital. You cannot even imagine the emotional trauma of being put back in there. I was finally back home with my kids where I belonged—now I would have to tell them I was leaving again for who knows how long.

Upon arriving at the hospital, they checked me back in and attempted to put an IV in my arm. All of my veins were collapsing and shrinking from having so many IVs in me for so long that they could not get an IV in me. They decided to insert a PICC line. It was a tube that would be inserted in the vein at my elbow and run all the way up to my heart. The nurse came in my room and attempted this procedure. It was excruciating! I had to make her stop trying after about the fifth attempt to force this tube into my vein. She did not appreciate that I wouldn't allow her to keep torturing me, and she was downright mean to me! I don't know what she noted in my chart, but every doctor or nurse that came in my room after that looked at my chart and said, "I see you refused the PICC line."

I did not refuse it! I allowed her to try several times; clearly, she was not going to get it!

The next morning, another nurse came in my room to attempt to insert the PICC line. She was so much nicer than the woman the night before. I explained to her what had happened when the other nurse tried.

She said, "Okay, let me take a shot at it."

I agreed to let her try.

She began inserting the tube in my arm and said, "No wonder she couldn't get it in, this tube is bigger than your vein."

She immediately stopped trying and went to talk to my doctor about how he wanted to proceed. They ended up taking me to surgery to insert the PICC line so it could be guided on a screen somehow. I was actually glad they chose to do the PICC line because it could be kept in the entire time I was in the hospital—unlike the IVs that had to be changed every three days at most, unless my veins would collapse before that.

Once they figured out how to get medicine directly in my system, they informed me that I would need another surgery on my right arm to close the wound that never healed. I don't know if they didn't tell me how they were going to do that or if I just didn't remember them telling me because I was on so many pain meds. I went in for surgery on my right arm. When I woke up from surgery, my right leg hurt extremely bad! My eyes weren't even open yet, and I said, "That f——en hurts!"

I heard a voice say, "Does it feel like your leg is on fire?"

I replied, "Yes, *why*?" to which she responded, "That's where they took the skin graft from."

I had no idea what she was talking about, and I was still heavily sedated. When I was fully awake and out of recovery, I discovered that the surgeon had to cut a large chunk of skin and meat out of my arm and transfer it to the incision that did not heal. He then took a skin graft off my leg to use as a human Band-Aid over the area that they removed the large chunk of skin and meat. I was so upset. I already had scars all over my body. This surgery gave me worse scars then the accident itself! I knew it was necessary, but that didn't make it any easier to accept mentally or emotionally.

I was in the hospital for a total of five days that time. I was happy to be out of there, but that skin graft was so painful. If I moved my leg at all, it was just severe pain! My arm looked so bad. I would not touch it, and I tried not to even look at it. Thank God for my mother and my sister. My mom would wash it for me when I took a shower. I would stick my arm out the shower curtain so she could wash it. My sister would come over every day and clean my wounds and change my bandages. I know I never would have gotten through this without God and my amazing family.

Chapter 6

BACK TO OUTPATIENT THERAPY

I had to get right back in therapy the day after I was released from the hospital. Five days a week, I would get up, be forced to eat breakfast, and take a ton of pills. My mom would get me dressed and ready to leave and then go to therapy. I would be basically tortured for an hour in physical therapy and then an hour in occupational therapy and then come home to sleep because my pain pills knocked me out. I was physically there when my kids came home from school, but mentally, I was in another world. I would try to help them with their homework, but my mind just couldn't do it. I don't know if it was all the medicine or if it was from the trauma of the accident. All I know is that I couldn't focus long enough to figure out elementary school math.

It was an extremely depressing time for me. Prior to the accident, my life revolved around my kids. Now I was sitting in a wheelchair, unable to care for myself, let alone my children. My husband and I were not getting along at all. He was absolutely no help to me when I got out of the hospital. My eleven-year-old daughter had to do my therapy for my arm because he would hurt me every single time I asked him to do it. She had to help me with showers and getting dressed because he would just walk away in the middle and let me sit there, unable to move myself. I remember sitting in my wheelchair, looking out the window one day, thinking, *How am I going to divorce my husband when God just saved my life?* I felt trapped in a body that wasn't working and in a marriage that wasn't working. However, I was determined that my children were not going to sit in that house all summer and look at me. They were going to have a great summer, even if it wasn't with me. Once again, my family came through. Everything my sisters did with their kids that summer, my kids were invited to join them.

I do not remember the exact time line after I was released from the hospital. But I do know that I had a total of six surgeries on my right arm and two surgeries on my left leg over a nineteen-month period. After each surgery, I would have therapy five days a week, then four, then three, then another surgery, and start back over at five days a week! My doctor would wake me up after each surgery, and he would be so amazed and excited with the results! He was an excellent surgeon, but I believe the real reason I had such miraculous results is because I had so many people praying for me and because God was guiding him! The nurses even commented to me about all the people gathered around my bed, praying for me. They thought it was awesome.

My parents stayed with me and helped me for the first three months after the accident. When they left, my children took over. Jess would do all of the girl things, like putting my hair in a ponytail and closing my bra for me. Jake would do anything else I needed. I will never forget how he would always get up early on days that it snowed so he could shovel a path to my car before getting on the school bus—without me ever asking him to do that. My children are both adults now, but they still help me with anything I ever need!

Chapter 7

WHY, GOD?

People have already asked me questions like "Why aren't you mad at God?" and "Why would God allow that to happen to you?"

I was never mad at God! Somehow, I was always able to look at the good that came out of this situation. I could always feel God's presence, and I could always see the amazing work he was doing to restore me! I believe that my children are better people because of going through this experience with me at such a young age. This accident restored relationships in my family because they saw how fast somebody could be gone!

During the nineteen months of therapy, I got to witness so many different people go through so many different things. It was amazing for me to watch how much people's perception of a situation effects their attitude. There was a nineteen-year-old young man who broke his neck diving into his swimming pool, which left him paralyzed from the neck down. But every day, he would come to therapy smiling. There was a man who was involved in an explosion at his work, which resulted in him being burned on over 90 percent of his body! He would come to therapy every day smiling and telling jokes! There were also people with extremely mild injuries that came in therapy twice a week, bitter and upset. I think I was somewhere in the middle. I was grateful to be alive and still have all my limbs attached! But if I thought too much about the woman who did this to me and then lied repeatedly to avoid taking responsibility for her actions, I was bitter and angry!

I believe it is important to pay attention to how you perceive things because that dictates how you will respond to them. If you allow Satan to make you focus on the negative in every situation, he will be happy to indulge you. Joyce Meyer says, "Where the mind goes, the man follows." And she is absolutely correct. I could have focused on all the negative things throughout this journey, and believe me, there were plenty to focus on. But instead of focusing on the pain, I focused on the progress. Instead of focusing on what I couldn't do, I focused on learning how to do it again. I focused on the promises of God's Word to get me through all of this.

As a matter of fact, focusing on God and the promises in his Word are how I get through my entire life, not just the accident. I talk to God all day every day! He is my best friend, my trusted protector, my great provider! I am actually grateful that he trusted me to go through all of this with him so I could have a miraculous testimony to tell others about the amazing power of prayer that he offers to sinners like me. Christians are not perfect; they are just forgiven!

"Vengeance is mine," says the Lord. It was my job to forgive; it is God's job to get vengeance.

Several years after the accident, a customer came into our auto repair shop and was telling us a story about his neighbor at his hunting cabin up in Bradford County.

I replied, "His wife is the one who almost killed me in the ATV accident."

His response amazed me. He told me how people always say, "Don't worry, they will get theirs." "But in your case, she did get hers. She was outside, burning garbage in a barrel, and she accidently started herself on fire. She spent three weeks in the burn unit of Lehigh Valley hospital."

Lehigh Valley Hospital is three hours away from her home. It is the same hospital I spent three weeks in after she almost killed me! Oddly enough, I wasn't happy to hear about her accident. I actually felt sorry for her. It is so sad to watch people go through life without Jesus and have to pay the penalty for their sins.

Chapter 8

THE PROPHECY

The woman who almost killed me the night before Mother's Day decided that it was a good idea to lie about absolutely every detail of the accident and sue me personally for fifty thousand dollars.

Upon impact with the Blazer, the front wheel of my ATV was completely torn off of the machine. There was damage to the undercarriage of her vehicle from running it over. The frame of the ATV was bent, and the handlebars were bent at a ninety-degree angle. Despite all of the physical evidence, she sat in a court of law under oath and told the jury how she was completely stopped and we just attacked her with our ATV and then left her there alone.

How a jury believed that, while unconscious and gurgling, I left on my three-wheeled four-wheeler still blows my mind today! Another thing I can never seem to figure out is how you can almost kill somebody and not care at all! It was just so easy for her to tell completely blatant lies throughout the entire legal process. She will have to answer to God for this. As a Christian, I am required to forgive her, and I have.

It did take several years for me to come to the place that I was able to forgive her, but I got there.

The only thing that I care to remember about the entire legal process was the day my twelve-year-old daughter told me the prophecy that Jesus had given her. I was extremely upset about all the lies and deception. I asked my daughter to pray that the truth would be revealed, and I would win that lawsuit. She came to me the next day and said, "Mom, you're not going to be happy. Jesus told me you are not going to win this time. But you are going to win next time."

"What is next time?" I replied. "There better never be a next time. If there is a next time, just leave me in the woods to die! I will never go through that kind of pain again."

We went to trial about a year later, and I lost. Immediately after the verdict, Jess looked at me and said, "Why are you upset, Mom? I told you, you weren't going to win today."

Sometimes, it is hard to have faith while waiting for God's timing. Sometimes, God's plans don't make sense in our minds, so we choose not to believe them. Fortunately, we serve an amazing God that is understanding and quick to forgive. Although I chose not to believe the prophecy because it didn't make sense to me, God was still faithful to complete his plans.

Chapter 9

THE MOTORCYCLE ACCIDENT

April 27, 2013, two weeks shy of ten years later, my husband and I decided to take the Harley for a ride to get dinner. We were planning on riding into New Jersey where they have a helmet law, so I went to the garage to get our helmets. When I arrived at the bike to give my husband his helmet, he said, "Let's stay in Pennsylvania, then we don't need the helmets."

I set both helmets down on the patio and got on the back of the motorcycle.

Since my ATV accident, I always make it a point to pray for God's hedge of protection around us every time I get on the bike—that day was no different. I prayed, and I had complete faith that God would keep us safe. About ten minutes into the ride, I felt my husband locked up the brakes and felt his body tense. I looked up and saw a car pulling out of a side road directly in front us. I was shocked! I thought, *There is no way God is going to let me get in another accident.* Then my husband and the girl driving the car made eye contact, and she stopped! I felt my husband's body relax, and he began the maneuver to ride around her car, which was now partly in the roadway. Surprisingly, she started driving again. At that point, there was no way around her! It was the calmest accident I was ever involved in. My husband said, "It's on," and I said, "I know."

When the car and the bike collided, my husband and I were both ejected from the bike. My husband was thrown into the hood of the car, then the windshield, and finally landed in the roadway. By God's grace, he had no broken bones. There was no blood at the scene. He was just extremely stiff and sore! Two years later, he was diagnosed with post-concussion syndrome and a mild traumatic brain injury due to the accident. But after several months of therapy, he is able to live a pretty normal life, with the exception of some extreme headache days and some confusion when trying to follow written instructions.

My experience was a little different than his. As soon as the bike hit the car, everything went black. I could not see anything. I felt my body hit the fender, then *I saw a flash of Jess at twelve years old saying, "You're going to win next time, Mom,"* then I felt what I thought was my husband rolling over the hood of the car with me, then I felt nothing against me. I knew I was flying through the air and headed for the asphalt road. I had no helmet on, and I could not see which part of my body was going to hit the road first so I could even attempt to use my arms to protect my head. I was just picturing my head smashing off of the road. I began begging God saying, "Please, Lord, do not let my head smash into this road! I do not want to die!"

Then I felt my head smash into my husband's stomach and bounce back up violently! I still could not see anything, but I knew I was lying in the middle of the roadway, and I had to get up in case cars were coming at me. I struggled to stand up. My vision slowly returned. I saw an empty field first. As I began to turn, I saw my husband lying in the road. He was in a daze, but his eyes were open, and there was no blood. I continued turning and saw the 750-pound motorcycle lodged in the radiator of the car so deeply that the front tire was not even touching the road. Then I saw the girl who hit us just standing by her car doing nothing to offer us assistance. She later told my husband she was having a bad day and she just was not paying attention.

My husband and I were both taken to the hospital by ambulance as a precaution because we were involved in a motorcycle accident with no helmets. As soon as they were done examining me, I went to my husband's hospital room, and the very first thing I asked him was, "How did you roll over that hood with me?"

He replied, "What are you talking about? I did not roll over the hood with you. But you did land on me."

So who did I feel against me while I was rolling over that hood? I can only imagine that it was Jesus, guiding my path and keeping me safe.

Some people may think that God did not answer my prayer about keeping his hedge of protection around me, but he did. We just had some miscommunication. When I said, "Keep me safe," I meant, "Don't let me bounce off any more vehicles." He allowed me to be in the accident, but he definitely had his hedge of protection around me!

There are so many details of this accident that defy the laws of physics. People in motorcycle accidents never fly in the same direction. The passenger always flies first because they have nothing solid to hold on to. My husband always weighs at least twenty pounds more than I do, and I should have flown farther than him. But somehow, we landed in the same spot, and he landed before me and was there to cushion my landing. That would be a whole lot of coincidence!

Remember my daughter's prophecy almost ten years earlier? I was in another accident, and I did win in court this time. The girl driving the car was only eighteen years old. But she told the truth, and she took responsibility for her actions! This was the exact opposite of the experience with the woman in her fifties who hit me on my ATV and lied through the entire process! I understand that accidents happen. Neither of these women intentionally hit me, but the one who told the truth and took responsibility for her actions made it possible for me to forgive not only her but the other woman who almost killed me.

Chapter 10

OVERCOMING
FEAR

I have been riding motorcycles and four-wheelers since I was five years old. I have had my motorcycle license since I was eighteen years old. I did not ride my own motorcycle for over ten years after my ATV accident. Not only could I not ride but I also couldn't even watch my kids ride motorcycles or ATVs without practically having a mental breakdown. My kids spent the weekend at my parents' house a couple years after my accident. My father taught them how to stand on the seat of the motorcycle while they were riding around the track by his home. He also taught them some other tricks that I probably chose to block out because I cannot remember what they were. When I arrived to pick them up, he was so excited. He said, "Look what your kids can do!"

We walked over to the track to watch them, and they slowly rode their motorcycles around the track. He said, "Why aren't they showing you the tricks I taught them?"

I laughed and said, "They are not going to do tricks while I'm watching! They know I will have a mental breakdown!"

Years later, I decided to go to church one Sunday, and the message was about overcoming fear, not allowing fear to control your life. When we got home from church, I happened to see the Harley in the garage, and I thought, "I'm not allowing fear to stop me from doing what I enjoy any longer."

I got the Harley out of the garage, and I was determined to overcome my fear. My body was literally shaking, and something in my subconscious did not allow me to lean to the right. I think this was a protective thing because my right arm was crushed in the ATV accident. I repeatedly rode that motorcycle around the block, forcing myself to lean a little further each time I made a right turn. Eventually, I felt comfortable enough to go for an actual ride. My husband got his Harley out of the garage, and we went for a ride together. I enjoyed every minute of it. I was angry with myself for allowing Satan to stop me from doing something I loved and steal my joy for such a long time.

A few months later, my husband and I went to Biketoberfest in Daytona Beach, Florida. We took the two Harleys with us so we could each ride our own. It was one of the best vacations we ever had. It just felt so good to be able to enjoy a Harley ride down the coast next to my husband. Every year prior to that, I would ride on the back of his motorcycle, which I also enjoy sometimes. But now, when I ride on the back of his bike, it's because I choose to, not because fear forces me to!

Don't allow Satan to use fear to control you and steal your joy! Jesus does not want you to live in fear. He wants you to be confident and step out in faith! To be completely honest, I also allowed fear to stop me from writing and publishing this book for many years. I knew several years ago that God was putting it on my heart to write this book and to use my experience to help others come to Jesus. I thought, *I can't write a book! I barely made it through English I and English II in college."* Faith should have told me that "you can do all things through Christ who strengthens us." If God puts something on your heart, he will always give you what you need to complete it!

"Be strong and of a good courage, fear not, nor be afraid of them: for the Lord thy God, he it is that doth go with thee; he will not fail thee, nor forsake thee" (Deuteronomy 31:6).

"Fear not: for I have redeemed thee, I have called thee by thy name, thou art mine" (Isaiah 43:1).

Chapter 11

UNWAVERING
FAITH

S o many wonderful things have come out of this horrific experience. After watching God work so many times and in so many ways, you develop faith that is unwavering. No matter how bad a situation may look, I never worry. I always have complete faith that God will work it out for the good. My husband gets annoyed with me at times when he thinks I don't care because I never worry about anything. I try to explain to him that I do care. I just know that worrying is like rocking in a rocking chair—it gives you something to do but gets you nowhere. The Bible tells us not to worry about anything but, in all things, trust in Jesus. I understand that most people have trouble with this until they experience firsthand the amazing power of prayer!

God has given me so many opportunities to share my testimony to help so many people over the years. The most surprising time was when I went to court with my niece to beg her way out of a speeding ticket. I believed we didn't have any chance of having the charges dropped unless we spoke with the cop before the hearing and he had mercy on her. We arrived at the court early and were waiting patiently for the officer to arrive. A few minutes later, another young man came in with his mother for the same purpose. Each of them had received a speeding ticket on their way home from college. His mother was not waiting patiently. She was being rude and complaining the entire time. I did not want her negativity to affect our case in any way, so I decided to go outside to wait. She followed us out the door! She was walking behind us, attempting to have a conversation with us. I did not want to be rude, but I also did not want to be associated with her when the officer came. Then she asked my niece if she had any weed. I said, "No, she does not have any weed. She is a good Christian girl. She does not smoke weed."

The woman then explained that her son gets her the good weed at college to help her with her pain and her medical issues. I knew right then that God had put her in my path for a reason. I showed her all of my scars and told her about my accident and the amazing power of prayer. I told her that the only permanent fix for her problems was Jesus and she needed to find a good Bible-believing church near her home.

She got this shocked look on her face and said, "I just got this card from a lady at the grocery store last week." She pulled the card out of her purse, and it was for a Bible-believing church near her house!

We went our separate ways after that, so I do not know how she is doing, but I do believe God was trying to get her attention. I was completely wrong about the officer having mercy—he wouldn't even look at us. But the judge, on the other hand, did have mercy, and he dropped the charges, and she left with a check in her hand for the entire amount of the fine. Sometimes, God puts you in a place at the right time so you can minister to others.

> If any of you lack wisdom, let him ask God, that giveth to all men liberally, and upbraideth not; and it shall be given him. But let him ask in faith, nothing wavering. For he that wavereth is like a wave of the sea driven with the wind and tossed. For let not that man think that he shall receive any thing of the Lord. A double minded man is unstable in all his ways. (James 1:5–8)

God is always faithful. If you have faith and you truly believe without wavering, God will answer your prayers according to his will. Scripture after scripture tells us that "because of their faith," God granted their request. The woman who needed healing touched Jesus's clothes, and he replied, "Because of your faith, you are healed." The paralyzed man who was lowered through the ceiling to get to Jesus because the crowd was too big to get in through the front door was healed because of his faith! I believe I received my gift of healing because of my faith, the faith of my family, and the faith of my children.

You don't always get your healing when you think you should. There are times that it takes weeks, months, or even years for God to answer your prayers. I am reminded of a time when I had bone fragments floating around in my knee. Occasionally, the bone fragments would get stuck in my kneecap, and the pain was excruciating! I would have to sit on the ground immediately and force my knee to bend and straighten at different angles until the bone fragment would pop out of the joint. I would pray and pray that God would heal this. I know I should have gone to the doctor and got the surgery to correct this. But after spending several weeks in the hospital, doctors and surgeries were not high on my priority list. After several months of this, I was sitting on my kitchen floor in severe pain, trying to get the bone fragment out of my joint, I heard a television preacher speaking about God's healing power. I began yelling at God, "I know you can heal me! What are you waiting for? I have complete faith that you can and will heal me!"

That night while sleeping, I rolled over in my bed. With every move, it sounded like a literal grinder grinding up the bone fragments in my knee. From that night on, there was never a time that the bone fragments got stuck in my knee-cap and gave me excruciating pain. They did still get stuck from time to time, but it was not nearly as painful, more of an inconvenience. When the smaller bone fragments got stuck, I just couldn't bear weight on that leg until I got them out. I did eventually have the surgery to have them removed.

Don't ever lose your faith! God is always faithful to finish the work he started in you, but it is always in his timing! God is never early, but he is also never too late!

Chapter 12

BLESSED WITH A GREAT FAMILY

I am truly blessed to have the amazing family I have. After my accident, I would have a mental breakdown every time I felt like I was out of control. I remember one incident when I was extremely grateful to have my loving, supportive, praying parents. It was Thanksgiving Day, and my parents were home for the holiday. My children and I wanted to go to my parents' house for the weekend, so we were going to leave after dinner and follow them the 150 miles to their house. When it was time to leave, my children and I weren't ready and my father did not want to wait, so I told them to just leave and I'd be fine driving up alone. Apparently, I did not look at the weather forecast and had no clue what I was in store for. We got about halfway through the trip when suddenly, the roads were a sheet of ice with a snow covering on top of it. I was literally crying and having panic attacks while driving down the road. I was seventy-five miles from home and seventy-five miles from my parents' house and did not know what to do! Should I turn around and try to go back? Should I just keep driving and try to make it there? While I was crying and praying, my poor kids were trying to figure out what was wrong with me when, suddenly, a car started passing me!

My kids said, "Look, Mom! It's pappy!"

I said, "That's not pappy. Pappy is way in front of us. He left way before we did."

But they were right! It was my parents! They must have known somehow that I would need them! I got them to pull over and said to my father, "Please take my kids! I don't want to kill them if I panic and lose control. Also, you have to let Mom drive with me. I need her to pray for me."

Of course they agreed, and I drove the rest of the trip with my children safely in my father's vehicle and my mother in my vehicle praying for me. I was never so surprised or relieved to see my parents. My father is generally very impatient. I would have never imagined him sitting on the side of the road for at least thirty minutes waiting for me. But God never gives you more than you can handle! He knew I would need my parents, and he put it on their hearts to wait for me.

So many people take their parents and their family for granted. I never do! I am constantly thanking Jesus for the amazing family that I was born into! You do not get to pick your family. If you are blessed to have a loving, supportive family that is always there for you, remember to thank Jesus for them. I believe you are especially blessed if you are born into a praying Christian family. Also, always do whatever it takes to keep all your relationships healthy. Don't allow Satan to steal your family from you while they are still on this earth! I see so many people give up relationships with family members over the stupidest little things. They never get that time back, and they miss out on so much joy and so many memories.

If you are not blessed with a good earthly family, don't lose hope! Every one of us is blessed to have a heavenly Father who loves us unconditionally. If you open your heart to him and ask the Holy Spirit into your life, he will always love you, always forgive you, always teach you, always provide for you, and always comfort you. God has a plan and a purpose for each one of us, and he always gives us the tools and the support to accomplish that purpose. Also, with God, all things are possible. You can pray for your family members, and over time and with God's help, they can change into the people you would be proud to call family.

Chapter 13

WE SERVE A PATIENT GOD

The most amazing story I ever heard about the amazing amount of patience God has with us was from my husband's grandpa, George. His grandma, Claire, is a Christian and prayed the prayer of salvation many years ago. But George never wanted to hear about God or the Bible. Each time we would go visit George and Claire, we somehow ended up having a conversation about God. George would not engage in the conversation, but I always noticed him listening and paying attention to what we were saying. Claire really wanted George to turn to Jesus, especially because they were both in their eighties, and she didn't know how much time he had left on this earth. I began praying that God would continue to draw George to him. After a couple of visits, each a few months apart, I finally got the opportunity to talk to George about his beliefs. The story he told me left me in complete amazement.

When George was a teenager, he went on a hunting trip with his father in Six Rivers National Forest, Trinity Alps, in Trinity County, California. They set up their camp at the end of a logging road, went their separate ways to hunt, and planned on meeting back at the camp a couple hours later. When George left to go hunting, he had his dog, his rifle, 10 bullets and a pack of matches. When he finished hunting for the day, he attempted to make his way back to the camp. But he couldn't find his way back to camp! He was searching for his family or his camp and could not find either. He knew he was lost when he kept coming back past the same spots.

He decided to find a place where he could spend the night and start a fire to stay warm. He wanted to shoot some shots from his gun, hoping that somebody would hear the shots and come find him, but he didn't want to waste his bullets because he didn't know how long he would be out there or if he would need protection from wild animals. He decided to shoot the gun, but nobody came to his rescue. They were hunting on the side of a mountain, so it was a steep slope. George found a tree that he could prop himself up against to sleep and prevent him from sliding down the hill.

The next day, he continued his search for his family or his camp, but again, he had no luck. He again fired shots from his gun in an attempt for somebody to hear it and come rescue him, but again, nobody came. To make things worse, it started raining. Now he was wet and cold with no food or water, and the wet wood made it impossible for him to start a fire for heat with only his one pack of matches. George found a dead tree lying on the ground and laid against it with bark covering him in an attempt to keep the rain from hitting him. He slept on the ground next to the tree that night.

Morning came after a long, cold night. Again, George attempted to find his family or a way out of the woods. He tried firing more gun shots, leaving him with only one bullet. He was soaking wet and hungry and weak and did not know which way to go to get to any civilization. He finally turned to God. He said, "God Almighty, I don't know whether you are real or not, and I wish I did. I don't know if you exist or not, but I think you do. I hope you hear me. I'm lost out here, and I'm not sure which way to go to find my camp. I'm going to ask you if there is any way you can show me to get out of here."

In the wee hours of the morning, he sat down on a log and noticed a tiny stream of water running down the hill to the river. It occurred to him that if he followed the water to the riverbed, he could find his way out of the woods. He continued to look for any small amounts of water running, and he continued to follow it. He found the riverbed. Because of the time of year, the riverbed was dry, and George could walk on it. In the great distance, he could see smoke rising out of the trees. He headed toward the smoke, walking down the dry riverbed. The closer he got, the more brazen it looked. He finally got to the building and saw a lot of horses outside. He walked in the door of the building, and there were forty men in there, preparing to go look for him! They said, "You're George! We were just preparing to go look for you again."

George could barely speak. He was cold and hungry and thirsty. They gave him food and water and heated him up and dried his clothing by the fire.

When George finished telling me this story, I said, "So you're telling me that you asked God to save you and he did save you, but you still don't believe?"

He then explained how he doesn't really know much of the Bible and he doesn't know if he believes it. I didn't want to pressure him, so I let it go until our next visit.

The next time we were going to visit was around Christmas time, so I bought gifts for George and Claire. I do have a head injury, and I forget a lot of things. I forgot both of their Christmas gifts at home and didn't realize it until we were quite a way into our 350-mile trip. We stopped at a truck stop to try to find good Christmas gifts for each of them. I found a very nice picture for Claire and an awesome book for George that explained every book of the Bible. I wasn't sure if George was going to appreciate his gift, but he loved it! He studied that book and three different versions of the Bible to see how much it changed during the translation.

A few months later, we returned to visit again. George was so excited to show me all the things he learned in the book and the Bibles. I was so happy to see how much he learned and how much he grew closer to God. I asked him if he ever prayed the prayer of salvation or if he wanted to. He told me he had not prayed for salvation, but he would like to. I had the privilege of praying with George and his family for George's salvation. Jesus waited seventy years for George to acknowledge what he did for him that day in the woods and to ask Jesus into his heart. I'm sure there was a party going on in heaven that day!

Three weeks after I wrote this, George went home to be with his heavenly father. He continued seeking God and studying his Word right up to his last days. Although George had cancer that spread throughout his body, he never appeared to be in extreme pain. God's grace got him through it, and he passed away peacefully. His family has peace knowing that he is in heaven now, and I will forever be grateful that I had a part in bringing him back to Jesus before it was too late.

Chapter 14

THE BLESSINGS

S o many blessings came out of this terrible event. I truly believe that going through this ordeal with me at such a young age helped shape my children into the wonderful adults they are today. They learned at a very early age to appreciate that they still had a mother. When other kids were going through their difficult teenage years and begin to be rude and disrespectful to their parents, my kids were not. They were always so respectful and so helpful to me. I honestly do not recall them ever telling me that they hated me or any of the other hurtful things some teenagers say to their parents. Other parents would ask me how I taught my kids to be like that. I would reply, "You just have to have a near-death experience the night before Mother's Day."

I still have a very close relationship with both of my children. I believe that God kept me on this earth so they could have a mother, and I take that responsibility very seriously. There is not anything I wouldn't do for them. I'm sure it isn't easy for them to deal with me. My head injury causes me to forget just about everything, and I get severe headaches that cause me to have to take medicine and go to bed almost immediately. But they never complain. They just love me and help me, and I will forever be grateful for that.

My daughter, Jessica, is the oldest. She is the most loving, caring, generous woman. She is happily married, has three children, two stepchildren, and one child on the way. But that does not stop her from being a blessing to anyone who God puts on her heart to help. She will put all of those kids in the car and go wherever God leads her. She is an amazing wife and mother to all of the children. She is an awesome example of a godly woman who loves unconditionally. In her spare time, she runs a notary business out of her home. But her husband and her children are always her priority. She knows God will provide for all of their needs.

Jessica has the gift of healing. Last year, I was in Florida when I fell and broke my foot. I went to the emergency room to get an X-ray. After looking at my bruised and swollen foot, the doctor stated, "Barring a miracle, you are going to need an orthopedic surgeon."

I was shocked by this statement because doctors don't generally mention or acknowledge miracles. He then sent me for an X-ray. The X-ray did not show the break at this time, but the doctor informed me that breaks don't always show up right away because of the severe swelling and that I should have it X-rayed again when I returned to Pennsylvania. When I left the emergency room, I called Jess and said, "I think you are supposed to pray for my foot to be healed. The doctor said, 'Barring a miracle.' Doctors don't mention miracles."

Jess prayed for me, and the next day, when I woke up, I was able to move my ankle and put some weight on my foot—both things I could not do the night before. I returned to Pennsylvania and went to my doctor's office to have my foot X-rayed again three days later. The doctor was amazed when he looked at the X-ray and could clearly see where it was broken but appeared to be healed. He asked me how long ago I broke it. I told him three days. He informed me that this was not the kind of break that you can walk on, but I assured him I could. So he gave me a boot to wear instead of crutches and told me to return in a week. The first few days, the boot worked great. But around the fifth day, the boot started hurting me every time I picked my foot up to take a step. My five-year-old grandson was at my house and almost stepped on my boot. I explained to him that my foot was broken and he had to be careful not to step on it. He immediately asked me if I wanted him to pray for me! Of course I said yes! He then informed me that you can't pray when it's light out, you have to wait till bedtime. So we waited, and when bedtime came, he prayed for my healing as well.

The next day, I woke up with absolutely no pain, no swelling, and no bruising. So I took the boot off! I was walking around my home barefoot nine days after breaking my foot. I went to my appointment the next day and informed my doctor that I was healed and I no longer needed his services for my foot. He was amazed. He made me walk around his office to show him that I could do it and I had no pain. He asked me how this was possible, and I told him that God healed me! But I'm not so sure if he believed how I was healed, but he could clearly see that I was healed. That's okay because I know that God healed me!

My son, Jacob, is sixteen months younger. He is smart, generous, and a hard worker. He is happily married with three children and one stepchild. He works full-time while going to school for an electrical degree. He is always helping people any way he can. He is an amazing husband and father and an excellent example of a God-fearing man that works hard to improve himself and provide for his family.

I prayed for years for God to give Jacob a good Christian wife. Three months after meeting Brielle, who was a Lutheran and never heard of being born again, she became pregnant with their first son. I went to the twenty-week ultrasound appointment with Brielle. After completing the hour-long ultrasound, a doctor took us in a room and informed us that the baby had aortic stenosis, an enlarged kidney and thickening of the skull, which indicated Down syndrome. Brielle informed the doctor that all the boys in her family were born with aortic stenosis. I immediately thought, *I am praying against this generational curse, and my grandson will be born perfectly formed.* I was not going to accept this generational curse. I could not wait to get out of this office to have my family and friends start praying for this baby's healing.

As soon as I could get out of that building, I called Jess and told her to send a group text to the family and have them pray for Jake's baby. I told her everything the doctor said about the baby's current condition. I also told her to meet me at my house in thirty minutes to lay hands on Brielle and pray for the baby's complete healing. When Brielle came out of the building, I informed her that the entire family was praying for her, that Jess was coming to pray for her, and that I was not accepting the generational curse on her baby. I briefly explained the power of prayer and how words have power. I told her that she had to have complete faith in God if she wanted his healing and that she was not allowed to speak any of those conditions on this baby. The Bible says that we should speak things as if they already are (Romans 4:17). Looking back, I'm sure that this was extremely difficult for her. So many people were so concerned about her and had so many questions about what the doctor told her, and she wasn't allowed to speak it on the baby.

When we arrived at home, Jess was there, waiting for us. We gathered around Brielle in my kitchen, laid hands on her, and prayed for complete healing of the baby inside her, and we prayed for any generational curses to be broken! We could all feel the presence of the Holy Spirit so strongly as we were crying out to God and believing in him for a miraculous healing. Brielle was amazing! She was willing to do anything to save her baby. She followed every biblical instruction any of us gave her.

Because her pregnancy was now considered high risk, the doctors began giving her ultrasounds frequently. Each ultrasound we went to, we got to watch the baby being healed in her womb! The first one showed that there was no longer an enlarged kidney. The thickening of the skull was never even mentioned again. With each subsequent ultrasound, we watched the aortic stenosis get smaller and smaller until it was no longer an issue. By the time Jayce was born, he was formed so perfectly in his mother's womb (Psalm 139:13) that it was not even considered a high-risk birth.

A short time later, Brielle became pregnant again with another boy. I could not help but wonder if God had simply healed Jayce or if he broke the generational curse as well. I could not wait for her twenty-week ultrasound to see if this baby was forming normally or if he, too, would have aortic stenosis like the boys in the family before him. Finally, we had the ultrasound, and everything looked great! James was born perfectly healthy with no complications. Shortly after that, Jonah came, also perfectly healthy. God is so good!

I'm not sure of the exact time that Brielle prayed to accept Jesus as her Savior. But I know she did. When Jacob married Brielle, shortly after Jayce was born, she was a good Christian woman, and she is a great wife and mother. Not only did Brielle pray to accept Jesus as her Savior, but she and Jake decided together to get baptized. They did not tell me they were doing this. Instead, they made it a surprise for me. That was the best surprise I ever received. You can read Brielle's testimony in her own words in the back of this book.

The other thing God blessed me with was an amazing Christian husband. The thing that drew him to our family was our commitment to God and the answers to prayer that he witnessed firsthand. He has wonderful relationships with both of my children and would do anything for either of them. We have been married for over ten years, and our relationship gets better with each passing year. It's like he was made just for me, but God waited until I was ready to put him in my life. It is incredible when you do what is right according to God's Word and then you watch his blessings flow over you in every area of your life.

If God would not have allowed me to get in this accident and go on this journey with him, I don't know if I would ever have had the kind of faith I have now. I don't know if I would have had the faith required to heal my foot or heal my grandson in his mother's womb. I don't know if my children would have become the amazing adults that they are today. I don't know if my family would be as close as we are if we never saw how quickly somebody that you love could be gone. But I do know that God works in mysterious ways and what Satan intends for harm, God uses for good (Genesis 50:20). I wouldn't change any of it.

Brielle's Testimony

D id you ever feel like you were not worthy of God's everlasting love? Same. That was me and to be honest, I questioned that for a long time. I did not grow up in the church. I barely knew anything about the Bible. I attended a UCC Church but only a handful of times. I have tattoos all over my body. I was also a sinner and have made plenty of mistakes in my life. I am still not perfect whatsoever, but I know now that Jesus loves me just the way I am!

Before I invited God into my life, this was what was happening: I had premarital sex, I had to finish my senior year of high school pregnant, and I gave birth to my beautiful daughter right after I turned eighteen. Eventually, I got married to her father. I got a tad out of control after I turned twenty-one and was rebelling because I was very unhappy with my life and, eventually, I got divorced by the age of twenty-two. I could go on and on about my past, but to be honest, my past helped contribute to me being the much better, happier person I am today. Every broken path eventually led me to him, our heavenly Father, and for that, I am extremely grateful. I prayed for what I have now.

At the age of twenty-three, God placed many challenges in my path. After going through a divorce and starting a new relationship with my now husband, I knew I never wanted to ever feel the hurt in a resentful way as I did in the past. Three months into our relationship, I became pregnant with our son, Jayce. Jacob was also learning what parenting was going to be like while helping me take care of my four-year-old daughter. Our relationship started to get a little rocky when I saw messages on his phone from other females, but this was how I was introduced to God. I actually told his mother about what was going on in our relationship, which, to be honest, was a first for me. She came up to her son's bedroom where I was lying down (physically and emotionally exhausted) and dropped a Bible, a notebook, books, and a pen on the bed. She started talking about Jesus. She told me about praying and the power of prayer, and she, most importantly, said some things that I did not expect—like I did not have to stay with her son and she would understand if I left!

Over the next few days, I started to develop a relationship with Jesus and prayed over Jacob and myself. I had no clue what I was doing, but I stayed, took his mother's advice on the books, and I read *Power of a Praying Wife*, *Love Must Be Tough*, and *Battlefield of the Mind*. (I actually read these books multiple times now, but back then, I remember praying about getting a relationship with God, praying to be a good mom, praying to be the wife/woman God wanted me to be!)

The night I had my first encounter with God, which changed my view of my relationship with Jacob—I don't remember the exact date, but I was pregnant, and Jake wanted to go out. When we returned home, a message popped up on his phone. Of course we argued again because it was yet again another female. I fell asleep crying, but I was not having a normal dream. It was blank, colorless, and all I heard was a voice. I questioned the voice many times to figure out that it was a message from God. It was like he was whispering/talking to me in my dream! He told me that if I wanted to make this relationship work, I needed to *trust* Jacob and to stop checking his phone. Eventually, I abided to his word, and Jacob stopped following Satan's lead.

When I was twenty weeks pregnant with Jayce, I had a twenty-week ultrasound, which I was so excited about. I wanted to see his chunky face and confirm he was a little boy. The appointment started out fine, but things took a turn, and this became one of the worst days of my life. You go to the office all excited to end up having to sit in room with someone who felt like Satan himself, being told Jayce could have aortic valve stenosis (which was my family's genetic curse in boys), a birth-defect thickening of the skull, which could result in Down syndrome, and that his kidney was enlarged. It was tough. I cried for days, and I had a hard time trusting God or even talking about it (because Sandy, Jacob's mother, told me that I had to have complete faith and that I was not allowed to speak it on him).

Jess, Jacob's sister, sent out a family group text to get everyone praying for our son. Jess also showed up at the house, and we all prayed over my son while he was in my womb. We felt the Holy Spirit working! I also found some comfort in my brother, who was actually born with aortic valve stenosis. He, on many occasions, reassured me that Jayce will be just fine! I had multiple ultrasounds after that, which were all stressful. Although we could clearly see the improvements on the monitor, the same woman (that I referred to as Satan) said the same thing—"Child will be born with aortic valve stenosis and an enlarged kidney." I also decided to change offices because every time I talked to the doctor who told me about Jayce, it would stress me out, and guess who appeared at my last ultrasound? *The same doctor*! Now I was preparing for the worst but praying for the best.

March 4, 2018—my very memorable birthing experience. And I want to share it with you all! I started to feel like

I was going into labor at home the night before, so we went to the hospital. I decided to go with natural childbirth after a negative experience with the epidural when I gave birth to my daughter, Khloe. I got to sit in a jacuzzi tub, take naps, and Jake's sister, Jess, turned out to be the best fake nurse/birthing coach I ever had. I'm pretty sure it was the first time my dad got to experience God's presence when he tried to leave because he couldn't watch me in pain, but Jake's mother and sister prayed for him, and he was able to stay for the delivery. Jayce was a *big* boy. I got his head out, but his shoulders were stuck. I was exhausted from pushing and in so much pain. I guess I was almost passing out—I do not remember. The last thing I remember was hugging Jake at the top of the bed. In between passing out, Jake went to see the baby coming out and swapped roles with Jess. When she noticed my eyes close and my body go limp, she slapped me in the face lightly to wake me, which resulted in me putting her into a headlock over the bed rail. We were both crying when the baby made his arrival, and I thought it was because he was just so cute. I later found out that I actually hurt her back—but after the laughter and tears, they took Jayce back for an ultrasound of his heart and kidneys.

Suddenly, I felt comforted. I prayed, and he returned in the little cart, all snuggled and swaddled up about an hour later. We named him Jayce Micah. We chose Jayce because it sort of sounded like Jake, and *Micah* because it means "who is like God." They said he had no birth defects, no enlarged kidney, and the aortic valve stenosis on the ultrasound did not look noticeable but needed to be rechecked by St. Christopher's Hospital in a week.

The dreaded week came. It was dreadful because I had to take him to this appointment alone. I got driven there by my dad's girlfriend, and because she was not immediate family, they did not let her go back with me. Jacob went on a preplanned vacation with his family to Florida, and I was having a very tough time with being without him. I cried when my baby cried, and he cried through the entire appointment. I cried every time they stuck a monitor to his tiny body, and I cried at the ultrasound because it was the same balloon-shaped object I've seen in the ultrasounds while I was pregnant. They deemed it livable for now but told me to immediately go to the hospital if his color started to turn blue. They told me that if that did not decrease and the valve did not open to at least 80 percent (but don't hold me to it because I was a wreck that day), then they would have to operate (balloon or open-heart). I scheduled my next appointment at the end of May. I also called my brother that day, and once again, he told me, "It is going to be fine! I've lived with this my whole life!"

I attempted not to speak about it anymore. I prayed for my son, but I also cried all-day long.

Easter was the first and last time my brother got to see my son, Jayce. It was also the last family function we would have together. I did not see his eyes light up so big since he held my daughter Khloe when she was born and his daughter Fiona. He fell in love with him the moment he met him. We had a good few hours together, cracking jokes on each other like normal, especially from me because he previously cut his finger with a potato peeler. This generally would not be a big deal, but he was also a bowler and had just gotten a sponsor. When we didn't see each other, we would text pretty often and talk on Facebook. He messaged me on my birthday (May 2) and on May 7, he liked one of my pictures. A few hours later, he passed away, and I never got to say goodbye.

He passed away six days after my birthday on May 8. My mother never had an autopsy performed on him to confirm, but they said it was sudden, and they believe that his stent from his aortic valve stenosis, which was placed shortly after his birth, lodged out. I was woken up a little after midnight by a call from my mom to inform me of his passing. I was about to breakdown during the conversation with her. I prayed to God to keep me as strong as he possibly could. And he did. He still does.

Two weeks later, I attended church at Bethany Wesleyan in Cherryville. I really *did not* want to go to church that day, but when Pastor Addington invites us, we attend! God was definitely working in church that day. I was destined to be there; God answered my prayers and gave me peace. He also comforted me about my brother's passing. The church service was about breaking generational curses. A scripture came onto the screen: "I will give you a new heart and put a new spirit in you; I will remove from you your heart of stone and give you a heart of flesh" (Ezekiel 36:26). I believed. I trusted. I gave it to God. The scripture from church gave me peace that, somehow, my brother's spirit is connected to my son's heart. The scripture in the Bible also means that when one turns to God for forgiveness of sins, one is also filled by the Holy Spirit. I also had Pastor Addington pray with my mom over the passing of my brother. It gave me some relief for her since I still cannot imagine what she was going through. My son had his heart appointment the following week, and the valve was opened to an extent where it did not require a balloon or surgery! They said he will be monitored yearly until age eight. God is amazing. Jayce has never had an issue! He is now three and a half years old.

In May of 2018, we were blessed with a house. We purchased our first home from my in-laws! It felt great to have a home of our own, especially because it seemed like my husband never wanted to move out! Then we found out we were expecting again! Another beautiful blessing from God! Long story short, I was pregnant with another *boy*! Remember my generational curse that I thought was broken? Nope. It tried sneaking back up on us. At my twenty-week ultrasound, our faith was tested once again when they told us this son would have a birth defect, an enlarged kidney, and aortic valve stenosis. This time though, I didn't cry. I didn't feel broken, and when the doctor asked if everything was all right because I was not talking, I simply replied with, "Yeah, I'm good. They told me my last son was going to have the same issues, and he's perfectly healthy."

From there on out, I stopped letting Satan attack me through my children. I learned last time to just get on Jacob's family message group, ask them to pray, and not talk about it anymore.

Jacob and I also decided, at this point, that it was time to get married! But we had something up our sleeves. First was our trip to Vegas. We got married, and even though I was pregnant, we were having the time of our lives with most of our friends and family there! It was so much fun! We said, "I do," on November 14, 2018, at the Chapel of Flowers. It was sentimental to pick that place. I love flowers and Flores (our last name) also means "flowers" in Spanish.

When we arrived home, we also wanted to declare Jesus as our Savior together, even though mentally, I knew I declared him as mine a few months prior and Jacob prayed to receive Jesus as his Savior when he was young. So we researched when the churches would have baptisms coming up, and there was one that Sunday at Life Church in Nazareth. My husband loves this church. It is also like a huge party, worshiping God and singing about it the whole time! That was why we chose to do it there. It felt right and fun. Sandy also talked about us getting baptized many times, so we had it up our sleeves to not even tell her. We surprised her and some family members that we invited along and declared Jesus as our Savior! It was truly an amazing experience, and I am glad we did it together as husband and wife. Pastor Addington also invited us to attend a marriage conference with him and his wife, Carla, at our local church, Bethany Wesleyan. We spent an entire day there and learned so much. I carried the notes from that event with me in my wallet for years.

Before I gave birth to our next son, we did have many ultrasounds once again. They eventually determined that he did not have a birth defect and that he had no more signs of aortic valve stenosis. We decided to name our next son, James Malachi. A very *strong* biblical name because our God has been so good to us! James in the Bible believed that Jesus was the son of God that was sent to save the people of their sins, and *Malachi* means "my messenger." On April 6, 2019, I had a very quick and easy labor with James. God was there the entire time—I'm sure of it. I came in smiling. I did my nails at eight centimeters dilated. I again had no pain medicine. I tried to relax. I told everyone to "shhh" because I was singing in my head (they were distracting my song) and just held on to the bed and pushed! He was beautiful. They did monitor his presumed kidney enlargement, but there was nothing wrong with it. He just needed to go to the bathroom! He was happy and healthy! Another true blessing from God. In 2019, God blessed us as a family and taught us in many ways. I will spare you all the details, but I will tell you one compliment that has stood out to me for a long time. I have been told by multiple people that they are impressed at how well Jacob and I work together as a team. "Two are better off than one, because together they can work more effectively. If one of them falls down, the other can help him up" (Ecclesiastes

4:9–12). I thank God every day for giving me a Christian husband! He is my best friend!

Year 2020 came along, and the pandemic hit. Honestly for me, it is not scary. I am at peace with it, and I believe when it's your time, then it's your time. God has a plan for everyone. But for me, I was set on having another baby. My husband, on the other hand, was not on board at first. Eventually, with a ton of begging, we began trying for our last baby. It didn't come as easy as I thought though. I knew I was ready to be a mom again, but God had a different timing. After trying for a month and being a day late with my period, I was extremely excited to take a pregnancy test! I was shocked when it said negative and, honestly, very disappointed. I ended up getting what every woman does and, the following month, tried again. God made me wait a month, and I truly believe it was to have a due date that was very close to my brother's birthday. It helped me focus on the good rather than the sorrow. Unlike others, I am actually very thankful for 2020. Year 2020 brought me so much joy and happiness.

Before I even knew the gender of our baby, I had my names picked out. God blessed us with, yet again, another *boy*! We, but mostly I, gave him the name Jonah Mateo-Grant. Yes, Jonah as in Jonah and the whale. And *Mateo*, being Spanish, even though we are not, means "gift of God." I hyphenated the middle name and gave him my brother's middle name, Grant. But things were different with this pregnancy. I was glowing, and in every ultrasound, there was no more crying—no more aortic valve stenosis present, no more birth defects in question, no more signs of an enlarged kidney. The generational curse of boys in my family having aortic valve stenosis was broken. The power of prayer worked! Even though I knew for some time now how great it was, it opened my eyes even more to help other people as well. Our family prayed for about twenty people this year, and we saw answers!

The birth of Jonah was long and hard. He was born during the pandemic, so none of our family members were permitted in the hospital. After several hours of labor pain, I wanted to give up. I even asked for an epidural (I did not have it with my other sons, and I was very against getting it after I had Khloe). But Jake told on me, Sandy and Jess called immediately, and they got the whole family praying. Instead of calling for an epidural, the nurse accidently code blued me, and every doctor ran into my room. Jake quickly hung up the phone, and within minutes, I had to push. No one at home knew I was pushing, but their prayers were highly effective. I pushed Jonah out within thirty seconds! He was happy, healthy, and the most perfect gift from God. He also looks identical to my brother's baby pictures.

I didn't want to skip out on my daughter since most of my testimony occurred after I had her. My daughter is nine years old now. I had her when I was eighteen, and I feel like, at times, we had to grow up together. She has seen me at the highest and lowest points of my life, but every day, I was there as her mom. Striving to be the best for her and to give her a good life are what got me where I am today. She is a true blessing from God. I pray heavily that my daughter can be inspired to seek all that God designed her to be! As of right now, she is a great cheerleader and friend! She is also an amazing big sister and help for Mom and Jake! She does like going to church. She likes vacation Bible school and the water slide events at our church. She's also into unicorns and mermaids—the typical girly things! She also likes to read the Bible, books—even Christian ones—and, of course, play LOL dolls. She also started learning what praying is all about!

I want to end my testimony by saying thank-you to God for giving me the best life, a faithful husband, a group of beautiful kids, supportive family, and friends who feel like family! Also, I want to remind everyone, that it is not always an easy journey, but it is worth it! God has taught me that we are not alone. If you are married, one thing God has taught me was to check myself! Instead of praying or asking him to change your husband, figure out if you are also part of the problem! God can redeem what has hurt us and make it beautiful! He is worthy, and trust me, he will give you greater than you ever dreamed about!

Pray about it. Trust him. Love him. Give it to God!

Lori and Glenn's Story

In the summer of 1981, after graduating from high school, I met the love of my life. I was seventeen; he was eighteen. We were instantly in love! We were only able to spend a very short time together before he had to leave for the military. He joined the Marine Corps on the day before we met. Had we met one day sooner, he more than likely would not have joined. Shortly before he left, we discovered that I was expecting. We went to Planned Parenthood for a free pregnancy test. We made a firm agreement before our appointment that no matter what the outcome, we would not have an abortion! We were in love and willing do whatever was necessary for the pregnancy and our future together.

We left the appointment completely broken! We could barely face one another as we confirmed that based on the information we had received from the Planned Parenthood representative, the best and most responsible choice we could make was to have an abortion. She explained to us how difficult it would be for us to provide properly for the child at our age and how the abortion was just the removal of tissue if we acted quickly. It was time for Glenn to leave for the military, so my friend took me to the appointment and paid for the abortion. It was a very hard and sad day for me.

I was one of five girls, and my mom spent endless hours in our basement doing laundry. A few days after the abortion, with a heavy heart, I went downstairs to talk to her about how she would feel about me having an abortion. I will never forget the conversation! My mom proceeded to tell me that I should never ever have an abortion because that is murder and I would never be forgiven! I didn't tell her that I already did it or I am sure the conversation would have been much different.

Sadly, if we had consulted with our parents, I was confident my mother would never have approved. However, no parental consent was required. At that time, I had a junior driver's license with a driving curfew, couldn't get into R-rated movies or purchase alcohol, but sadly, I could make a life-altering decision that would end my unborn baby's life and alter mine forever—all based on the persuasion of a profit-making stranger! This was a tragedy in my life! A decision we would live to regret! I am confident we would have had a beautiful and perfect baby just like the four beautiful perfect girls we have now. I am also confident that we would have been able to provide well for him or her; instead, we suffered loss and pain. We were lied to and misled by Planned Parenthood. We are looking forward to the day we will meet our child when we enter heaven's gates under the precious care of Jesus. What a glorious day that will be!

After boot camp in Parris Island and schooling in Camp Lejeune, Glenn came home in May so we could get married! He only had a short leave, so we had to act quickly. We planned our wedding in ten days' notice! It was just a normal day. I remember my dad coming home from work to quickly shower for our Thursday evening wedding at our Lutheran church. I was dressed in my fifteen-dollar, simple, white wedding dress, which I bought at Fashion Bug. The only guests were my four sisters and his four sisters and boyfriends, a few of my aunts, our parents, best man, and maid of honor. Glenn got lost on the way to the church and was late for the wedding! We all met afterward at the Covered Bridge Inn in Palmerton for a dinner and homemade wedding cake his sister Denise made. A simple wedding that has been forty years strong!

Days later, Glenn was in an airplane headed to the California deserts of Twentynine Palms. He left his family, new wife, and beautiful green mountains of Pennsylvania to find himself in a dry, hot desert alone. He found an apartment in town for us weeks later and flew home to Pennsylvania to get me. We drove across the country in our little 1974 Mercury Capri, towing his dirt bike with a hitch he and my dad welded to the rear bumper to attach directly to the front forks of the bike without the front tire. With the motorcycle attached to the back of the car, it appeared as though the bike was pushing the car! It was quite the spectacle and drew a lot of attention. Our new life adventure together would begin in the California sun! The one strength that has always kept our marriage strong was our shared passion for fitness. We were living the dream, working out every night after work, partying on the weekends, and riding dirt bike in the desert. We were happy. We were in love and together!

After two years in California, Glenn got his orders to go on an unaccompanied tour to Okinawa, Japan! At this point in my life, Glenn was my whole world! He was my everything! I was troubled knowing that we would be apart for a year! Where would I live! What would I do? I worked at a Western Auto store in town, and a girl at work noticed my distress. She approached me and told me that she could see I was upset but she was also a military wife and had to be separated from her husband as well, but she told me that she knew Jesus! He was with her, and he helped her. She offered to teach me about him and invited me to a Bible class. This was the first time I heard anyone say the name of

Jesus outside of the church walls. I asked her how much it would cost for me to take the class. She assured me it was free and that her Bible study teacher would come to my house! I was excited!

We were moving in a few weeks, so there wasn't much time for her to teach us. I excitedly announced to Glenn that a lady was coming to our house to teach us about God and the Bible! He didn't share my enthusiasm! He was angry and said there was no way he was going to listen to some Holy Roller Bible study teacher! He was going to the gym! When Mary Cook arrived at our house, Glenn was not happy. She was a single mother. I believe she was Mexican, with beautiful long, black hair and a passion and fire for Jesus. She came several nights a week to finish the Bible course, "God's Plan for Man," before we had to move. Every time she came, Glenn would shoot questions at her like, "Why did God accept Abel's offering and not Cain's? He wasn't fair!" Glenn had read a few chapters of the Bible, and it just didn't make sense!

Mary wasn't moved at all by his questions and seemed to welcome them. She always had a good answer for every question. Glenn would go off to the gym while I listened to each lesson and did my homework. He was very interested and curious. Mary was telling us things we had never heard of before! She shared how God was doing miracles and healing people, and she told us about the Holy Spirit and speaking in tongues! Mary invited us to her Pentecostal Church for a baptism service. I wanted to go, but it was all too strange and scary for Glenn. I soon realized that Glenn started reading my lesson book and was several chapters ahead of me! Then he started sitting in with us. We were amazed at all the things she was teaching us. She would show us everything in the

Bible and taught us that all truth comes from the Word and must be confirmed in the Scripture.

She taught us how to pray! Every time she would come, she would ask one of us if we would like to open or close in prayer. We said no! But she would ever so gently guide us and tell us what to say. She told us to just speak out loud and ask God to keep his hand upon us and be with us. Just a simple sentence prayer. She prayed for us and explained the gospel message to us!

I invited Mary because I wanted information and help with my anxiety and fears about Glenn leaving, but at the same time, I felt extremely uncomfortable knowing that I clearly was a sinner, a murderer actually! I killed my baby! I had a strong feeling of unworthiness, guilt, and shame. I told Mary that I didn't think God could or would forgive me and that I didn't feel comfortable approaching him. I felt rejected by God!

Mary dispelled the devil's lies! She told me how Jesus loves me and how he died on the cross for the purpose of the forgiveness of my sin. She told me that if I was the only person on the earth, he still would have given his life as a ransom for me! I could hardly believe it was true! He really loved me. He forgave me, and he wanted to fill me with his Spirit. I was ready to declare him Lord of my life.

Honestly, it was a little hard to conceive all this new information! I remember being angry with her because she told me that unless a man be born again, he will not enter the kingdom of heaven. She taught us what the Bible said about being saved by faith and not works. She told us that even people who are good, like firefighters and community and family servants, cannot enter heaven unless they are born again. This didn't sit well with me. I was explaining to her that none of my family was born again and confronted her saying, "Are you telling me that if my grandfather wasn't born again, he wasn't going to heaven?"

She quietly and gently told us what the truth of God's Word said. She explained that if he did believe that Jesus died for his sins and confessed him as Lord, he would be saved. She assured me that my best course of action was to be sure that I was in right standing with God and share the truth of his love to everyone I love so that we can one day all be in heaven together. Even though it made us a little uncomfortable at first, somehow, we just knew it really was God's truth. We had been in church before and even read some parts of the Bible, but there was a missing link! That link was the Holy Spirit. No one had ever told us about being filled with the Holy Spirit!

Mary came to us with the living, active Word of God! Before we prayed with Mary and invited the Holy Spirit into our lives, we were spiritually dead. When we tried to read the Bible or pray, we were dead in our sins and living by the flesh and trying to please God by doing good works, which by the way is futile! As the Word says, "There is none without sin, all have sinned and fall short of the glory of God." Mary prayed for us that we would have a hunger and thirst for God's Word and that we would receive Jesus as our Lord and Savior and be born again. After confessing our sin and receiving Christ's forgiveness and declaring him Lord of our lives, we became new. We are forever grateful for her witness to us, and we know she will be rewarded in heaven for her part in our salvation. Our lives would never again be the same! Our time with Mary came quickly to a close as did the first two years of our marriage together in California.

We loaded our Ryder truck in the middle of a sandstorm in Twentynine Palms and headed back to Pennsylvania where I would stay with family while Glenn traveled overseas. We drove across the country, but this time, we were changed! We were spiritually alive and desired the Word of God. When a baby is born, he desires milk. I personally believe this is a true test in knowing if you are saved. When you pray and ask the Holy Spirit to fill you, something changes in you, and you develop a hunger and thirst for the things of God, and somehow, sin isn't so fun anymore! Because now, the Spirit of the living God is dwelling inside of you.

On our trip back to Pennsylvania, we took turns driving and reading the Bible all the way home! We were so full of the presence and power of God by the time we got home—it was incredible! Our first stop was at my sister and brother-in-law, Deb and Tim's house. We were brand-new Christians, but we could immediately sense the spiritual warfare taking place when we arrived there and began telling them about our experience with Jesus.

This was only the beginning of the miraculous work God intended to do in and through us and our family. While in Pennsylvania, I connected with another military wife, Sandy. We had become good friends in Twentynine Palms. Her husband, Dave, was also in Okinawa, and he got an apartment in town so she could join him. I immediately called Glenn and asked if I could come be with him. So he found a little hooch apartment for us, and I was on my way!

One week after I arrived, Glenn got orders to go to Korea. Again, we only had a short time for him to get me settled in before he left. I had to get a driver's license, and we bought a car with the steering wheel on the other side. I had access to the base, but living in town, we had no phone and didn't speak the language of the locals. I finally arrived in Okinawa, only to find myself alone as Glenn went to Korea.

After he left, I was lying on my bed in our very tiny first-floor apartment with paper-thin windows, reading my Bible when I heard a ruckus going on right outside my bedroom window. It was two marines having a fight over who was going first into the next-door apartment, which, I later realized, was the home of a prostitute. I could see and hear them. They were obviously drinking and cursing at each other and fighting. I was very afraid and, immediately, reached to turn off my light in hopes that they would not see an American woman through the window. I was terrified; I could feel my heartbeat racing and pumping through my chest. I was alone and afraid, with no phone and no way of escaping. But thank God! Mary taught me how to pray! This was the first time I prayed for real! I wasn't just mouthing or repeating words—I was, for real, praying! I was scared out of my wits! Amazingly, I repeated the words Mary Cook taught me to say, "Dear God, please keep me in your protective hands!" I prayed passionately! As I prayed for the first time in my life, I experienced the presence of God like never before! He really was with me—immediately. Like a flood, his peace came over me! I fell into a deep and restful peace and slept through the night. The next morning, I awoke, giving thanks and praise to my God who was with me and in me, who protected me and gave me peace. From that point on, I knew that God is alive and well! He is! This was my first experience of the power of the Holy Spirit to answer the prayer of faith and fill the room with his presence. How awesome and real!

Glenn was going through his own struggles during his time in Korea. He really enjoyed the cooler weather there. The frost in the mornings reminded him of Pennsylvania. They had a base camp with huge tents that held twenty to thirty men. They did drills, shooting the M60 machine guns in the field, setting up camo netting to hide the trucks, etc. In the evening, they went out to the small town on liberty trucks that held about a dozen or more marines. Out in town, it was full of night clubs, beer, and girls. Three dollars would get you a young girl all night. They had a big billboard at camp that had each club and how many men got STDs from each. A needle symbolized a dozen cases. They warned them to stay away from the worst clubs. Glenn had prayed and given his life to Jesus earlier in California, but he still drank beer with his buddies. One night in a small club, he and his buddy got pretty drunk and ended up in the back bedrooms (a blanket on the floor) with a couple of young girls. Something sobered him up really quick, as he felt a very strong conviction that he needed to get out! He literally ran out of the room through the bar through the village to the liberty truck to head back to camp. The rest of the time on the tour, he focused on keeping his trucks maintained. He was a 3521 mechanic, studying his Bible and Marine Corps manual for a board his officer recommended him for, out of his unit, to compete against top marines from other units for the rank of Sergeant E-3. He went in front of the board (officers from each unit that drilled him with questions, etc.), and he won!

He meritoriously received the rank of sergeant and, at the end of his tour, received the commanding general's letter of recognition for his outstanding upkeep of the unit's fleet of jeeps and trucks. Looking back, Glenn feels that his tour of duty was a test of his newfound faith and walk with Jesus. This was his forty days in the wilderness experience. Glenn feels confident that the Holy Spirit within him helped him overcome his temptations and focus on good, and he was rewarded!

Some scriptures he learned later on in his walk with God:

Temptation—
No temptation has overtaken you that is not common to man, God is faithful, and He will not let you be tempted beyond what you can bear. But when you are tempted, he will also provide a way out so you can endure it. (1 Corinthians 10:13 NIV)

Youthful Lusts—
Flee also youthful lust; but pursue righteousness faith love and peace, along with those who call on the Lord out of a pure heart. (2 Timothy 2:22 NIV)

Reward—
And without faith it is impossible to please God, because anyone who comes to him must believe that he exists and that he rewards those who earnestly seek him. (Hebrews 11:16 NIV)

I am so grateful that we were able to find Christ when we were young and newly married. I am confident our marriage would never have lasted without the power of God working in and speaking truth to our hearts. Glenn and I both have strong-willed personalities. Our marriage has certainly not been without struggle but never without the help and blessing of the Lord. We give God all the glory for sustaining and blessing our marriage. Like Sandy said, "He took us all the way to California to bring us to himself." I don't even want to imagine what our lives would be like if we would have continued living in the ways of the flesh and the world.

We were so fortunate to have found Christ early in life. I was in Okinawa, Japan, when I turned twenty-one. I didn't go to twenty-one bars and have twenty-one drinks! Instead, I found myself in God's house, worshiping my loving Father. I had been sneaking into bars, using a fake ID since I was seventeen. I couldn't wait to be of drinking age. But thank God, I was now a new creation in Christ, and my life would have a completely different outcome.

God filled us with a passion and hunger for his Word. In Okinawa, we went to church every Wednesday night and went to a Bible study with a missionary in town. We learned so much!

We never had a TV. We spent all our free time studying the Word, in the gym, or on the beach.

God used the time that we were away with the military to establish us in our faith and the Word. One year later, we returned to Pennsylvania, wondering if a church existed that taught about the Spirit-filled life and the Word of God. We were at a family event and shocked to learn that two of Glenn's fellow high school graduates, the most unlikely of all people, started telling us about their Bible study! We couldn't believe it! It was four or five couples our age who would meet every week in an elderly woman's home, and we loved it! We didn't miss a week in two years. We learned so much! Our teacher was Leah Sheckler. We will be forever grateful that she made it her business to provide a way for young couples to grow and learn in the Lord.

We also found a church. It turned out that there actually was a church that taught born-again salvation only a few minutes away from our house. Sandy Koch told us about her Wesleyan Church in Cherryville with Pastor Dwight Addington. We have never met a humbler man of God with a passion for people, families, and Christ, with his wife, Carla. Under his teaching, preaching, praying, and the power of the Holy Spirit, we were able to witness one, at a time, the conversion of our loving family members to Christ! Starting with my mom and sister Deb. We will never forget the Sunday on Father's Day when my brother-in-law Tim answered the call to the altar and gave his life to Jesus. Glenn's sister, Cheryl, also committed her life to the Lord while attending this church with us. Every Sunday, we filled several pews with our newly saved family members.

We eventually moved to Palmerton, Pennsylvania, where we were so fortunate to have Pastor Rick Collins pay a visit to our house. As he was walking around the block and praying one day, he invited us to his church around the corner from where we lived. This was an experience like no other! It was a full-gospel, uncompromised, Word-preaching church. I remember experiencing the presence of God the moment we walked in. We could barely hold back our tears! The presence of God was so tangible! The perfect place to raise a godly family. Pastor Rick and his wife, Nancy, were also raising four girls. He was a great teacher and student of the Word. He taught us so much! We can never thank him enough for the impact his teaching and life has had on us. He committed himself to reading and praying and studying and then he taught! Being the recipient of his teaching has absolutely transformed our world. We attended and served the Blue Mountain Community Church as we raised our four girls—Angela, Nicole, Vanessa, and Kayla—who all love, know, and serve Jesus! Thank you, Pastor Rick, and thank you, Jesus!

Since then, we have discovered so many amazing ministries in our area and online.

To think there are so many powerful people and ministries of God all around us, transforming lives, giving people hope and life-healing prosperity, making disciples of all nations! I, like so many people around me, was living in darkness, completely unaware of the great love and saving grace of our heavenly Father. I didn't know I could be loved, forgiven, filled with his Spirit, become a new creation of God, born again, happy, prosperous, and blessed. I didn't know! Until someone told me!

Go into all the world and teach the gospel to every creature. He that believes and is baptized shall be saved!

About the Author

Sandra Valentino is a new author who captivates her audience with the story of her miraculous healing. The most important thing in her life is her relationship with Jesus, closely followed by her family. She is blessed to be able to spend every day with her two adult children and six grandchildren. She is also blessed with an amazing husband who always supports her.

Reach Out to the Author sandyv.comeasyouare@gmail.com

- * Reach Out to share how this book has impacted your life.
- * Reach Out to request helpful resources as you continue on in your journey.

CPSIA information can be obtained
at www.ICGtesting.com
Printed in the USA
BVHW040256290323
661285BV00002B/296